Publisher's Preface

Robert Gallagher
Publisher
Saint Benedict Press, LLC
TAN Books

Over the course of our spiritual journey, we sometimes travel high on the peaks of divine consolations and sometimes struggle to find God in the valleys filled with obstacles and difficulties. The saints who experienced these "dark nights" remind us that God allows the valleys and obstacles in order to teach us to rely more and more on Him, and less and less on ourselves. This booklet introduces you to St. John of the Cross's writings so that you will be encouraged and strengthened, before and during your sojourn through the valley of shadows.

The Classics Made Simple series aims to introduce the great works of Catholic literature to a wide readership. The Classics of the Faith are not meant only for saints and scholars: they're meant for everyone. They're wise, human, practical, and they have something important to say to each of us.

The Classics are also timeless. Other books come and go, passing with the tastes and fads of each generation. But the Catholic Classics remain and God has used them to teach and sanctify men and women of every age.

We hope this *TAN Guide* will stir within you a desire to read *Dark Night of the Soul*, or if you've already read it, to re-read it with a renewed interest. You'll discover each *TAN Guide* is a perfect vehicle to introduce your newest favorite Classic to your friends and family. Give this little booklet a few minutes of your time and see what happens!

"The dark night is a certain inflowing of God into the soul which cleanses it of its ignorances and imperfections, habitual, natural, and spiritual."
—St. John of the Cross

Introduction to—*Dark Night of the Soul*

Dark Night of the Soul is a brief work, but one that deeply challenges its readers with its rich exploration of the minute stages of advancement in the spiritual life. It is a great spiritual Classic that has illuminated the understanding of many and will continue to inspire those who read and re-read it.

During a period of imprisonment at the hands of those who opposed his religious reforms, St. John of the Cross (1542-1591) wrote a body of spiritual poems. Later he wrote treatises explaining his poems, two of which, *Ascent of Mount Carmel* and *Dark Night of the Soul* (which supplement each other and together form a joint treatise on mystical theology), explore his poem that begins "In a dark night . . ." In the poem, the "beloved" soul sings of its journey toward the "lover"—Who is God. Through this language of love, each stanza poetically describes the process of purgation, spiritual enlightenment, and finally union with the Divine.

The Need for Purification

It is vital to approach *Dark Night of the Soul* with the understanding that the call to contemplation is universal because the call to salvation is universal. All people are made to share eternal life with God; contemplation is simply a seed of that eternal life experienced during earthly life. Union with God is the proper goal of each and every one of us, whether we attain it by His grace or fail to attain it by our attachment to sin.

Because of the universal call to sanctity, St. John's meticulous exploration of the stages of spiritual growth applies to all of us. It is not simply written for monks and nuns; every human being is called to greater love and holiness.

But this does not mean that we are ready for immediate union with God. Because of sin (original and personal) each of us has a host of discordant and rotten things that must be rooted out of our souls before perfect union can be attained. Growth in the spiritual life is like that of an athlete, requiring rigorous training and self-discipline. Sin is like physical injury or an illness from which the soul must recover. An injury such as a broken leg could require physical therapy before the athlete returns to his full strength, just as a disease may require surgery before a patient recovers health and energy. This can be a very painful process. Nevertheless, an athlete cannot run a race well unless he is well-trained and all his limbs are whole. In the same way, there can be no spiritual growth, no attainment of our ultimate goal of life with God, without purification—whether in this life or the next.

The Stages of the Spiritual Life

According to St. John, the spiritual life progresses through three definite stages: that of the beginner (who strives to meditate on the mysteries of God) followed by an experience called the Dark Night of Sense; that of the proficient (who achieves contemplation) followed by the Dark Night of the Spirit; and finally that of the perfect (who enjoys a divine union with God). Throughout all three, the soul endeavors to grow in virtue, to root out sin, and to display a growing openness toward God. The virtues necessary to defeat the deadly sins are manifested in a particular way in each stage.

The Way of the Beginner

The soul's first impulse toward God is not strong enough to raise the soul to Heaven. For beginners (into which class most readers of *Dark Night* fall), love of God is still in its early stages. The beginner does not yet love God perfectly; he lacks proper self-discipline and retains attachments to a number of sins and earthly things. His house is not yet "in order," as St. John's poem puts it. There is need for growth both in self-knowledge and in knowledge of God. What beloved would not want to become more intimately acquainted with his Lover?

To achieve self-discipline, the beginner has to undergo mortification and thorough purification. Moreover, even as he makes progress spiritually, he has to avoid or struggle through a number of

---

Renaissance, Revolution, and Reform

1521

Portuguese explorer Ferdinand Magellan becomes the first sailor to circumnavigate the globe.

1533

King Henry VIII of England divorces Catherine of Aragon, marries Anne Boleyn, and is excommunicated. In 1534 he decrees the Act of Supremacy, making himself the head of the Church in England.

June 24, 1542
John de Yepes born at Hontoveres in Old Castile (now Spain).

pitfalls particular to this stage. To a large degree, the beginner at this stage is governed by his passions and appetites. These need to be properly ordered and regulated before he can make any progress. In like manner, his imagination, memory, will, and intellect must all be purified and reordered. This process will bring about the healing of the soul from many sins, including pride and *acedia* (spiritual sloth).

All the while, the beginner is very much encouraged by the sweetness of abundant spiritual consolations, especially if he has habitual recourse to the sacraments, including frequent Communion and Confession. Overall, the beginner needs to desire to be led by God into the "dark night" of purification. He must recognize that he cannot achieve perfection on his own and that his own efforts

at mortification can only go so far. When the spiritual capital sins are removed—which is a very difficult and a painful process—the soul is fit for the first "dark night."

The Dark Night of Sense

The first dark night is much more commonly experienced than the second, but they are both painful. The Dark Night of Sense is a period of passive purgation during which the soul experiences trials given to it directly by God. These trials primarily, but not exclusively, take the form of interior suffering and involve (among other thing) the weaning of the soul off of the sweet milk of spiritual consolations experienced by the beginner. By endeavoring to grow in virtue and to root out all sin, the beginner has begun the process of purification. He has done as much as he can in

1543

Copernicus publishes his theory that the Earth and the other planets orbit around the Sun; the Copernican Revolution forever changes astronomy and, ultimately, all science.

1545

In response to the Protestant Reformation, Pope Paul III convenes the Council of Trent, which confirms the Canon of the Bible, reforms the clergy and the liturgy, and promotes religious instruction.

1567
John is ordained a priest.

1563
John receives the Carmelite habit and takes the name John of St. Matthias.

cooperation with God's grace; now God steps in to do His own work in the soul, continuing the process of purification.

The soul in this dark night is not melancholic or tepid, though such physical and psychological conditions can be mistaken for this spiritual state. The soul is "passive" during this stage of purification—but it is vital to recognize that a "passive" soul is not static or unconscious. On the contrary, the soul continues to cooperate with God's purifying agency, submitting itself utterly to Him. Most importantly, during this dark night the soul's appetites are reordered so that instead of loving spiritual consolations received from God, he will come to love God Himself.

The Way of the Proficient
The soul of the proficient enjoys greater freedom, abandon, satisfaction, and joy after its purification. The lover's house is "at rest," his senses have been purified and reordered, and he has been refashioned by the Beloved. The proficient rejoices that he no longer simply loves the creature, but loves the Creator, abandoning the goods of God for the Good of God Himself. He no longer labors toward meditation; his soul rises to joyful contemplation. Now, after his experience of suffering, he truly loves.

The benefits that come in the wake of the dark night are innumerable: the experience of infused contemplation, an increased knowledge of self and of sin, greater reverence for God, spiritual illumination, and a growth—if not an amplification—of all the virtues, including humility, love of neighbor, docility, liberty

Renaissance, Revolution, and Reform

1568
John of the Cross, as he is now called, initiates reform among the Carmelite friars.

1577
John of the Cross is taken prisoner for defying his provincial and endures nine months of torture in a narrow cell in Toledo; during this time he receives heavenly consolations and writes poetry.

December 14, 1591
St. John of the Cross dies at the age of forty-nine.

1582

The Gregorian Calendar, named for Pope Gregory XIII, is established and eventually adopted in most countries.

of spirit, spiritual purity, spiritual sobriety, spiritual temperance, holy fear of God, patience, love, peace, and gentleness. Through growth in virtue and the grace of God, the soul is endowed with the twelve fruits of the Holy Spirit. The proficient is largely delivered from the world, the flesh, and the devil, and grows daily in eager desire to serve God.

It is not to be assumed, of course, that those who pass from the stage of the beginner to that of the proficient no longer need to struggle against sin or strive to grow in virtue. On the contrary, as the soul becomes closer to God, sin becomes all the more repulsive. This is because, in the growing intensity with which we recognize the inexpressible perfection of God, the full horror of the smallest of our imperfections is revealed with increasing clarity. Moreover, the proficient is plagued by his own particular set of sins, all of which are closely related to the habitual imperfections of the beginner. The beginner struggled against the twining vine of sin, and now the proficient battles with the roots of those sins. He can easily fall into self-deception, pride, and presumption. He still lacks perfection, therefore further purification is necessary.

The Dark Night of the Spirit

The second dark night, that of the spirit, is experienced by very few souls, and is much more awful to the spirit. This dark night, even more compellingly than the first, represents a form of purgatory experienced on earth. Just as the Dark Night of Sense was sent by God to raise the beginner to higher things and purify the senses by reordering and subjecting them to the spirit, the Dark Night of

---

1619
St. John's writings, including *The Ascent of Mount Carmel* and *The Dark Night of the Soul*, are published for the first time in Barcelona.

THE
Tragicall Historie of
HAMLET,
Prince of Denmarke.

By William Shakespeare.

Newly imprinted and enlarged to almost as much againe as it was, according to the true and perfect Coppie.

AT LONDON,
Printed by I.R. for N.L. and are to be sold at his shoppe under Saint Dunstons Church in Fleetstreet. 1605.

1601

William Shakespeare's *Hamlet* premieres at the Globe Theatre in London.

1620

Dutch-man Cornelis Drebbel invents the earliest human-powered submarine; these diving vessels will contribute greatly to stealth warfare and underwater exploration in centuries to come.

the Spirit is sent to unite the soul ever more closely to God through even deeper purification. To understand this, St. John's explanation of the "dark night" metaphor is particularly important: the "darkness" of the night is not owing to God's absence, but to His proximity. The blindness of the soul is not owing to an absence of light, but to its abundance. In this dark night, the soul is once again purified and more effectively subdued to God's will, becoming ever more perfectly disposed for union with God in love.

During the Dark Night of the Spirit, the will is passive except in consenting and attending to God's action within the soul. The pain of this dark night arises because of the meeting of contraries: the darkness of the soul revealed in the light of God; the weakness of the self contrasting with the strength of God; the loss of God felt in the soul's consciousness of its unworthiness; the emptiness of the soul felt in contrast to the fullness of God; the memory of past happiness now in contrast to intense suffering; and the soul's inability to fix its attention properly on God.

The Way of the Perfect

The Dark Night of Sense purified the appetites and re-ordered the senses; the Dark Night of the Spirit purified sense and spirit together. From this second dark night comes the infused wisdom of love enjoyed by the perfect. The soul's house is now truly and fully "at rest"— the person's flesh is at rest with his spirit and his spirit is at rest with God. As the soul increases in holiness, it advances in knowledge and experiences extraordinary joy in the union of its illuminated intellect and purified will with

Renaissance, Revolution, and Reform

1674

Anton Van Leeuwenhoek is the first to see and describe bacteria with a microscope; imaging in the biological and medical sciences begins.

December 27, 1726
St. John of the Cross canonized by Pope Benedict XIII.

God. Meanwhile its experience of love becomes all the more glorious. The soul of the perfect is indeed like the soul of a lover, inebriated, and emboldened by love. Now, armed with the three theological virtues (the breastplate of faith protecting him against the devil, the helmet of hope protecting him against the world, and the royal robe of charity shielding him against the flesh), he is ready to venture forth into the darkness and into the welcoming arms of the Beloved.

Night More Lovely than the Dawn

In his *Dark Night*, St. John truly combines the poetic and the scholastic; he is as meticulous in his theology as he is ruthless in identifying the degrees and effects of sin. But the work remains a portrait of the lover as he quests for His beloved, suffering through the fires of purification and purgation so that his love will be transformed and elevated. Man, properly ordered, desires God above all things, but the path toward spiritual perfection is a difficult one, as St. John knew from his own experience. No man can complete the journey of sanctification without God.

Few readers of St. John of the Cross will attain the last stage of spiritual perfection in this life; in no way is *Dark Night of the Soul* a how-to manual for experiencing mystical prayer in a few easy steps. It is a challenging book, and often intimidating, but this should not discourage. Rather it should inspire beginners to take up their own crosses and start on a slow and careful way up the path of purification and growth. ◆

DID YOU KNOW?

The body of St. John of the Cross remains largely incorrupt after many centuries, despite having once been packed in lime to speed its decomposition.

Into the Night of Sense

An excerpt from *Dark Night of the Soul*

But the behavior of these beginners on the way of God is not noble, and very much according to their own liking and self-love, as I have said before. Meanwhile, God seeks to raise them higher, to draw them out of this miserable manner of loving to a higher state of the love of God, to deliver them from the low usage of the senses and meditation whereby they seek after God, as I said before, in ways so miserable and so unworthy of Him. He seeks to place them in the way of the spirit wherein they may the more abundantly, and more free from imperfections, commune with God now that they have been for some time tried in the way of goodness, persevering in meditation and prayer, and because of the sweetness they found therein have withdrawn their affections from the things of this world, and gained a certain spiritual strength in God, whereby they in some measure curb their love of the creature, and are able, for the love of God, to carry a slight burden of dryness, without going back to that more pleasant time when their spiritual exercises abounded in delights, and when the sun

of the divine graces shone, as they think, more clearly upon them. God is now changing that light into darkness, and sealing up the door of the fountain of the sweet spiritual waters, which they tasted in God as often and as long as they wished.

God thus leaves them in darkness so great that they know not whither to betake themselves with their imaginations and reflections of sense. They cannot advance a single step in meditation, as before, the inward sense now being overwhelmed in this night, and abandoned to dryness so great that they have no more any joy or sweetness in their spiritual exercises, as they had before; and in their place they find nothing but insipidity and bitterness. For, as I said before, God now, looking upon them as somewhat grown in grace, weans them from the breasts that they may become strong, and cast their swaddling-clothes aside: He carries them in His arms no longer, and shows them how to walk alone. All this is strange to them, for all things seem to go against them.

Recollected persons enter the dark night sooner than others, after they have begun their spiritual course; because they are kept at a greater distance from the occasions of falling away, and because they correct more quickly their worldly desires, which is necessary in order to begin to enter the blessed night of sense. ◆

The Life of St. John of the Cross

John de Yepes was born June 24, 1524, in Hontoveros, in the Spanish region of Old Castile. His father, Gonzalo de Yepes, was an impoverished silk weaver, who had been disinherited by his family when he married a woman below their rank. Gonzalo died young, leaving his widow to support the family, aided by her eldest son.

John, the youngest, did well at school in Medina del Campo, but was less successful when made an artisan's apprentice. Instead of continuing as an artisan, therefore, he worked for ten years at the hospital of Medina amongst the poor and suffering, while at the same time continuing his studies at a school founded by the Jesuits. Throughout his youth, he treated his body with severe mortifications and devoted himself to prayer and self-sacrifice. While in prayer, he received a mission to serve God within a religious order and to help bring back the ancient perfection of that order.

Carmel and Reform

On February 24, 1563, John received the habit of the Carmelites and entered their house in Medina, taking the name of John of St. Matthias. Soon he began to yearn for a more rigorous observance of the Rule (the monastic precepts by which religious live). Over the years, popes had granted dispensations and mitigations to the Carmelite Rule, but John wanted to embrace it in its original form. He

St. Teresa of Avila, prioress of the Convent of the Incarnation in Avila

June 24, 1542	—John de Yepes born in Hontoveros, Spain
1567	—Ordained a Carmelite priest
1568	—Founds first Discalced Carmelite friary in Duruelo
December 1577	—Taken prisoner by Carmelites who oppose his reform; escapes the following August
December 14, 1591	—Dies at the age of forty-nine
1726	—Canonized by Benedixt XIII; named a Doctor of the Church 200 years later

received special permission from his superiors to do so.

John continued his studies at Salamanca and in 1567 was ordained a priest. He was overwhelmed by the secular responsibilities of the priesthood and soon felt a desire to join the Carthusians (an order of enclosed monks who live together as hermits). Before he could do so, however, he met St. Teresa of Jesus, a Carmelite nun and reformer.

Teresa persuaded John to remain with the Carmelites and to help her in founding a monastery of friars who would live according to the original Rule. With two companions, John established the first household of "Discalced" (shoeless) Carmelites near one of Teresa's convents in Villadolid on November 28, 1568, changing his name to John of the Cross.

The Dark Night of Persecution

When Teresa was elected prioress of the Convent of the Incarnation in Avila, she called on John to serve as director and confessor for the nuns, which he did for over five years. Meanwhile their reforms to the Rule had begun to make them enemies among those who wished to preserve the status quo, leading to troubles and persecutions for Teresa and John.

In early December 1577, John was taken prisoner by his former Carmelite brethren and imprisoned for over nine months in a cell in Toledo. During his imprisonment he suffered greatly and was tortured but received heavenly consolations. He composed much of his poetry during this time.

After a dramatic escape (by fashioning a rope from blankets, climbing out the window, and scaling

Biography

The Life of St. John of the Cross

down the walls of his prison) in August 1578, John went on to found a number of Discalced Carmelite monasteries throughout Spain. When St. Teresa died on October 4, 1582, John supported her nuns in the continuing internal struggles of the order, defending their desire not to be assimilated into the larger government of the order. He was once again punished for his efforts and was removed from his offices and sent to one of the poorest monasteries in the order, where he fell gravely ill. The persecutions continued until his death on December 14, 1591, in Ubeda, Andalusia.

After his death, St. John's followers and admirers testified to his holiness, eventually gaining respect and honor for his memory. St. John's works were first published in 1619 and he was canonized on December 27, 1726. His body, resting in a gilded coffin for veneration at a Carmelite church in Segovia, remains miraculously incorrupt to this day. ◆

Carmelite Friars

The *Real* Dark Night

It can be tempting to see every significant hardship or suffering as a direct experience of the "Dark Night" described by St. John of the Cross. The term is casually thrown around in secular use and has even become familiar in Catholic parlance, oftentimes without understanding.

A careful distinction has to be made between the kind of suffering that results from sin, the suffering that comes in the course of more general purification and the particular purgation and affliction that characterize a true spiritual dark night. The most compelling testimony to the reality and the profundity of the Dark Night comes in the writings of the saints, who describe years (and sometimes decades) of passive purification. The greatest sufferers are usually the most silent—not least among them Blessed Mother Teresa of Calcutta, whose posthumously published writings revealed her own Dark Night, which lasted for nearly fifty years.

Remember that the Dark Night is not for spiritual beginners, but for those already advanced in holiness. For although the "darkness" St. John describes does indeed often involve the withdrawal of spiritual consolations, this is a characteristic of any growth in the nearness of God: the closer we stand to His Light, the more it blinds and overwhelms us. The Light ever more clearly illuminates our own appalling sinfulness and unworthiness, but such self-knowledge is a necessary component of a growing knowledge of and intimacy with God—a union which brings indestructible joy, even in the midst of any darkness. ◆

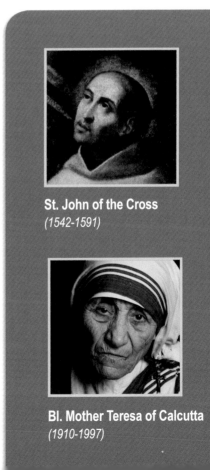

St. John of the Cross
(1542-1591)

Bl. Mother Teresa of Calcutta
(1910-1997)

Poets, Lovers, and Mystics

The tradition of religious poetry—particularly love poetry—has a long and honorable pedigree, beginning before the time of Christ and extending beyond St. John of the Cross into the present day.

The Song of Songs

Like the *Psalms*, the *Song of Songs* (or "Canticle of Canticles"), historically attributed to King Solomon, uses the language of courtship analogically: the lover's relationship with his beloved is symbolic of the relationship between God and the soul (the chosen "bride" of God). Even further, along with the *Psalms,* this Old Testament book demonstrates the way that poetry, as a surging expression of the heart, can work to express something as inexpressible as our love for God. This is one of the reasons that Old Testament poetry, and particularly *Song of Songs*, has greatly influenced many mystics throughout Church history. St. John of the Cross, for example, not only turned to the *Psalms* repeatedly in his writings, but also wrote a paraphrase of *Song of Songs* in his "Spiritual Canticle."

St. Thomas Aquinas

The mystical tradition and its affinity to poetry can also be seen in medieval theologians. The "Angelic Doctor," a Dominican friar known primarily for his extraordinary philosophical and theological works, St. Thomas was also the author of exquisite liturgical hymns, each of which poignantly gestures toward the Eucharistic mystery. Commissioned by Pope Urban IV to compose an Office for the Feast of Corpus Christi (established in 1264), St. Thomas produced hymns that are still sung today. It is popularly believed that the Franciscan St. Bonaventure was given the same task, but when he heard St. Thomas's work recited, was so moved by its beauty that he tore up his own attempt.

St. Francis of Assisi

The founder of the Franciscan Order and one of history's most popular saints, St. Francis of Assisi composed his "Canticle of the Sun" (also known as the *Laudes Creaturarum* or "Praise of the Creatures") as a hymn in praise of all creatures, and through them, of the Creator. In his loving delight, St. Francis even goes so far as to praise "Sister Bodily Death": "Happy those she finds doing your most holy will," he writes, "th   ~ond death can do no   .nem." This joyful work is unquestionably recognized as the work of St. Francis, unlike the popular "Prayer of St. Francis" ("Make me a channel of your peace . . .") whose authorship is questionable. "Canticle of the Sun" is filled with love for the Creator, and the saint's humility and mystical understanding of the greatness of God shine through each line. ◆

The Mother and the Confessor

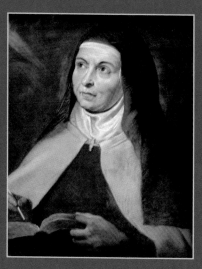

*St. Teresa of Avila
(1515-1582)*

When St. John of the Cross first met the formidable Teresa of Jesus, foundress of the Discalced Carmelites, he was seriously considering exchanging the Carmelite habit for that of the Carthusians. Recently ordained to the priesthood, he felt overwhelmed by his own unworthiness for that office and he yearned for a religious life according to a stricter rule with increased prayer, solitude, and purification. Teresa did not discourage his aspirations to such a life, but she showed him that he could embrace it as a Carmelite.

Renewing the Rule of the Carmelites was a special fulfillment of Teresa's spiritual aspirations. Born in 1515, the daughter of a pious family, she had first entered the religious life out of a feeling that it was the safest route for a young woman who was (in her own estimation) prone to sin. Over the years, however, and through many painful and serious illnesses, she became deeply prayerful and developed a profound understanding of the stages of mental prayer. She received "intellectual visions and locutions" which disquieted her and even made her notorious for a time, until confessors and advisors came forward who recognized the handiwork of God. Throughout, she suffered from a sense of her own unworthiness and sinfulness—a struggle to which John of the Cross could perfectly relate.

Eager to find a more perfect way of life, Teresa founded the convent

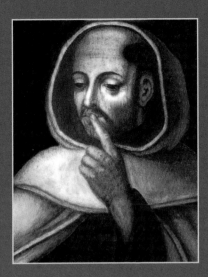

*St. John of the Cross
(1542-1591)*

of Discalced Carmelite Nuns of the Primitive Rule of St. Joseph at Avila in 1562. Over the next few years, she established several more convents (despite persecution from her fellow Carmelites). When she met John in 1567, she was eager to establish her reform among the friars as well. In John of the Cross, she had found an equally passionate reformer and together they persevered through more trials and persecutions.

The influence of Teresa on John was indeed extraordinary; among other things, Teresa taught him joy,

which she considered an integral part of daily life within her communities. But theirs was not the one-sided relationship of a lady patron exerting her authority over a grateful protégé. On the contrary, Teresa often submitted herself to John's authority as a confessor, despite the fact that she was over twice his age at their first meeting (he was twenty-five, she was fifty-two). During John's time in Avila, their closeness grew and became a deep spiritual friendship, which greatly informed their mystical understanding. Their conversations were so wonderfully fruitful and full of God that at one time they were seen to have gone into a state at ecstasy in the midst of a conversation—and to levitate together.

So deep was their affection that it might be said when, in 1926, St. John of the Cross was named a Doctor of the Church ("The Mystical Doctor"), his achievement was not complete until 1970 when St. Teresa joined him as the first woman declared a Doctor of the Church. She was honored further with the title: "Teresa of Avila, Teacher of Prayer." ◆

$\mathcal{S}$trong $\mathcal{R}$oots

St. John of the Cross's Spiritual Influences

SCRIPTURE

Lamentations 3:44
"Thou hast wrapped thyself with a cloud so that no prayer can pass through."

Lamentations 1:13
"From on high he sent fire; into my bones he made it descend; he spread a net for my feet; he turned me back; he has left me stunned, faint all day long."

Isaiah 58:10
"If you pour yourself out for the hungry and satisfy the desire of the afflicted, then shall your light rise in the darkness and your gloom be as the noonday."

Psalms 62:3
"How long will you set upon a man to shatter him, all of you, like a leaning wall, a tottering fence?"

Psalms 73:21-22
"When my soul was embittered, when I was pricked in heart, I was stupid and ignorant, I was like a beast toward thee."

Matthew 7:14
"For the gate is narrow and the way is hard, that leads to life, and those who find it are few."

The depth of St. John of the Cross's mystical vision was derived from his spiritual formation: in the *strong roots of faith* that lie beneath the surface for every Catholic Classic and every great saint. What were some of his strong roots?

The School of Suffering

St. John's description of the stages of the spiritual life corresponds closely to those of other saints, but this is not because he studied their work directly. Many have described his work and that of St. Teresa of Avila as "empirical" or experienced mysticism, which begins not in study but in personal experience.

Both within the monastery and outside it, while he was serving the nuns of St. Teresa or living in community with his brethren, St. John dedicated himself to self-sacrifice, fasting and especially to mental prayer. He challenged himself to purge all imperfections from his soul and to develop virtues. His description of the Dark Night is that of a man who has suffered through it. Thus it can be said that some of his most vital "roots" came from the day-to-day experience of the Carmelite life.

The Liturgy of the Hours

The cycle of prayers recited daily at particular hours makes up an integral part of the life of the Church, particularly life in religious orders. For St. John of the Cross, the Liturgy provided a frequent avenue to Sacred Scripture (especially the *Psalms*) and to selections from the writings of the Church Fathers. Through the Liturgy of the Hours (also called the Divine Office), St. John regularly encountered the writings of a host of great saints and spiritual writers (including Dionysius the Pseudo-Areopagite, St. Augustine, St. Gregory, St. Bernard, and St. Bonaventure) whose works he does not seem to have read on their own. Every day he would return to the Scriptures and every day he would more completely internalize what he read, particularly the writings of the Old Testament prophets, so that quotations and paraphrasing flow seamlessly from his pen.

The *Summa Theologiæ*

St. Thomas Aquinas's magnificent and vast opus—which was drafted as a manual for beginners!—is another work that St. John seems to have internalized. His knowledge of the *Summa* is staggering; in fact, his understanding of the spiritual life would not have been possible without the structure provided by St. Thomas, particularly in his theological explanation of the virtues and the gifts of the Holy Spirit.

This emphasis on the virtues is appropriate for St. John, for the "darkness" of his text is not owing to the absence of God, but rather shows our blindness when gazing upon Him from an ever closer range. For both the Angelic Doctor and St. John, as indeed for all saints, the goal is the same: union with God in the Beatific Vision. ◆

The Carmelites

Contemplative prayer is the special charism of the Carmelite Order and can be discerned even from the order's earliest roots. Drawing on the tradition of the Old Testament prophets, especially Elijah and Elisha, the example set by St. John the Baptist, and by Jesus Christ Himself, Christian men went into the desert and adopted lives of prayer and mortification. These men were rigorous as hermits in their solitude yet, at the same time, they often lived like monks in a community. They followed the example of their Jewish forefathers in honoring Mount Carmel as a place of spiritual pilgrimage and holy hermitage.

Such are the spiritual origins of the Carmelite Order, which, from its formal foundation during the thirteenth century, placed special emphasis on the importance of mental prayer, silence, and solitude. The Carmelite movement had existed for some time; during the first millennium, Christian hermits built a chapel on Mount Carmel and dedicated it to Our Lady. Their migration to Europe in the thirteenth century, however, brought many challenges, primarily that of adjusting the life of the desert hermit to urban conditions. All of this influenced the development of the "Rule" by which the Carmelite communities were to live. Further modifications came under the guidance of St. Simon Stock (c.1165–1265), who sought to settle the order in its new home in Europe, altering the Carmelites' focus from a primarily monastic observation to a mendicant way of

life—they became "begging friars" alongside the recently founded Franciscan and Dominican orders. The Discalced Carmelite observance, formed by St. Teresa of Avila and St. John of the Cross, returned to the older and more strictly monastic version of the Rule.

By 1274, when the Carmelite Order was approved at the Second Council of Lyons, its habit, or distinctive dress, was firmly established: a mantle of pure white wool was added to their brown tunic, scapular, and hood, earning them the nickname "Whitefriars" to distinguish them from the Blackfriars (Dominicans) and Grayfriars (Franciscans). More importantly, the Carmelite aptitude in a new school of religious thought—mystical theology—was formed. A life of daily mental prayer, fasting, and penance was ideal for the development of an intense spiritual life: so much so that mystical theology came to be recognized as a special province of the Carmelites, crowned by the work of St. Teresa, St. John of the Cross and, later, St. Thérèse of Lisieux. ◆

DID YOU KNOW?

When he was a young boy, St. John of the Cross was saved from drowning by the miraculous intercession of the Virgin Mary.

Mount Carmel

Good Fruits

The Legacy of St. John of the Cross

For some time after his death, the work of St. John of the Cross was largely neglected, even by his fellow Carmelites. At the beginning of the nineteenth century, his writings experienced a significant surge in popularity and went on to influence many nineteenth- and twentieth-century writers in a profound way: from his fellow Carmelites (St. Thérèse of Lisieux and St. Teresa Benedicta of the Cross) to non-Catholic writers such as the poet T. S. Eliot. His profound influence on two of the most prominent Catholic figures of the last 200 years is demonstrated in their writings and even more compellingly in their lives.

St. Thérèse of Lisieux
(1873–1897)

"Ah!" declares St. Thérèse of Lisieux in her autobiography, "how many lights have I not drawn from the works of our holy Father, St. John of the Cross!" The influence of St. John of the Cross can indeed be seen in her work, though she does not frequently reference his writings. St. Thérèse suffered deeply for many years from the withdrawal of all spiritual consolations—her own "night of nothingness," during which her faith and her love were sorely tested. In the end, St. Thérèse can be seen as a little champion of her Carmelite brother. Her devotion to him came when he was only just beginning to be read once again by Catholics and particularly by his fellow Carmelites.

Bl. Pope John Paul II
(1920–2005)

Blessed Pope John Paul II not only wrote a doctoral dissertation on the spirituality of St. John of the Cross, but chose to take the name of that great Doctor of the Church upon his election to the papacy. "From the first years of my priestly formation," he wrote, "I found in him a sure guide in the ways of faith. This aspect of his doctrine seemed to me to be of vital importance to every Christian, especially in a trail-blazing age like our own which is also filled with risks and temptations in the sphere of faith." The Holy Father's admiration for the saint bore special fruit in his own work in the mystical theological tradition, his poetic writings, and in particular in his passionate devotion to the Cross and to Jesus Christ crucified.

"The hand of God, so soft and gentle, is felt to be so heavy and oppressive, though neither pressing nor resting on it, but merely touching it, and that, too, most mercifully; for He touches the soul not to chastise it, but to load it with His graces."

—St. John of the Cross

How to Read *Dark Night of the Soul*

A Catholic Classic is not like other books. Properly read and meditated upon, it nourishes not only the mind but the soul: effecting in the reader an increase in *holiness* as well as knowledge. Follow this guide, based on the advice of St. Alphonsus Liguori, to get the maximum benefit from *Dark Night of the Soul.*

First, set aside a quiet place and time. Novels and newspapers can be read on the bus or in a noisy house, but not a Catholic Classic. Pray before you begin, asking God to teach you the lessons He wants you to learn. Ask for St. John to be present, praying for and with you.

Have the right intentions. The purpose of spiritual reading is to grow in love of God and divine things, not to acquire facts, learn arguments, or indulge superficial curiosity. We shouldn't read a Classic just to say we have read it; we should read it because we want to be changed by it.

Read slowly and with attention. Like food that must be chewed carefully, spiritual reading requires some work in order to draw out its nutrients. Don't be afraid to linger over passages, prayerfully re-reading sections that confuse you or make a strong impression on you. Let's be like bees, says St. Alphonsus, who "do not pass from one flower to another until they have gathered all the nectar they found in the first."

Finally, come away from your reading time with some concrete intention **to take what you've learned and put it into practice.** Having received the spiritual wisdom of the saints, carry it with you in your heart, and put it to work in service of God and neighbor.

Stanzas of the Soul

I.

In a dark night,
With anxious love inflamed,
O, happy lot!
Forth unobserved I went,
My house being now at rest.

II.

In darkness and in safety,
By the secret ladder, disguised,
O, happy lot!
In darkness and concealment,
My house being now at rest.

III.

In that happy night,
In secret, seen of none,
Seeing nought myself,
Without other light
or guide
Save that which in my heart
was burning.

IV.

That light guided me
More surely than the
noonday sun
To the place where He was
waiting for me,
Whom I knew well,
And where none appeared.

V.

O, guiding night;
O, night more lovely
than the dawn;
O, night that hast united
The lover with His beloved,
And changed her into her love.

VI.

On my flowery bosom,
Kept whole for Him alone,
There He reposed and slept;
And I cherished Him,
and the waving
Of the cedars fanned Him.

VII.

As His hair floated in the breeze
That from the turret blew,
He struck me on the neck
With His gentle hand,
And all sensation left me.

VIII.

I continued in oblivion lost,
My head was
resting on my love;
Lost to all things and myself,
And, amid the lilies forgotten,
Threw all my cares away.

The Nine Stages of Prayer

The great mystics and masters of prayer, such as St. John of the Cross and St. Teresa of Avila, recognized nine stages of prayer. The nine stages divided into categories of ascetical prayer and mystical prayer represent grades of spiritual elevation, ascending toward the perfection of mystical union with God.

ASCETICAL PRAYER: Prayer initiated by man in which the soul works to acquire virtue and self-discipline, and through them cooperates with God.

Purgative Way (Beginners)
I. Vocal Prayer: Prayers spoken or written, expressed either in public (as in liturgical prayer) or in private, arousing man's devotion and attention.

II. Discursive Meditation: Similar in its origins to the study of religious truths, a prayer which begins when the intellect is applied to a supernatural truth, from which reasoned consideration flows an act of love.

III. Affective Prayer: A simplified form of meditation in which the will (in loving) predominates rather than the intellect (in reasoning), deepening the soul's union with God through acts of love, often bringing with it great sweetness and spiritual consolations.

IV. Acquired Recollection (or the Prayer of Simplicity): A prayer of simple gaze, in which the acts of the intellect and the will are simplified and combined into a simple, loving attentiveness to the presence of God and to the truths of the Faith.

Dark Night of the Senses: A period in which the senses undergo purification, particularly through the withdrawal of spiritual consolations.

MYSTICAL PRAYER: Prayer initiated by God in which the intellect and will are passively receptive to Him and the soul is directly transformed by Him.

Illuminative Way (Proficients)

V. Infused Contemplation: Loving knowledge that is not the result of discursive reason (the intellect is captivated by God), but is intuitive, and is only possible through the operation of the gifts of the Holy Spirit.

VI. Prayer of Quiet: Intimate awareness of God's presence that is not prompted by the soul, but is infused by God with great sweetness and delight.

Dark Night of the Spirit: A period in which the soul undergoes continued purgation which purifies the soul for perfect mystical union with God.

Unitive Way (The Perfect)

VII. Simple Union (or the Prayer of Union): Prayer in which all internal faculties (will, intellect, memory, and imagination) are captivated by God, and the Divine Reality is so intensely experienced that the soul often falls into ecstasy.

VIII. Conforming Union (or Spiritual Betrothal): A deepening intensity in which God unites Himself to the soul in a mystical union while the soul continues to experience purifications and purgations in preparation for mystical marriage.

IX. Transforming Union (or Spiritual Marriage): The highest degree of perfection that can be attained on earth, characterized by the transformation of the soul in God, mutual surrender of the soul to God (as Beloved and Lover), and a permanent union of love prefiguring the experience of the Beatific Vision.

Words to Know

Appetites: Internal human tendencies or inclinations (neither good nor bad in themselves).

Asceticism: A spiritual tradition emphasizing self-discipline and practice of spiritual exercises for the sake of growth in virtue.

Consolation: A sweet assurance of the presence and love of God, benevolently endowed upon a soul by the grace of the Holy Spirit.

Contemplation: A stage of prayer in which God captivates intellect and will, and infuses the soul with a loving knowledge of Him.

Discalced Carmelites: (Literally, "shoeless.") A branch of a religious order founded in the twelfth century, reformed by St. Teresa of Avila and St. John of the Cross in the sixteenth, with a mystical charism and a strict rule of life dedicated to mental prayer.

Doctor of the Church: One of the thirty-three officially recognized master teachers in the history of the Catholic Church.

Meditation: A stage of prayer in which the intellect focuses on a religious truth, prompting a loving surge of the heart toward God.

Mystical Theology: The branch of theology that addresses the acts and experiences of the soul which are brought about solely through the action of divine grace and not through human efforts—the realm of "mysterious" experiences in the spiritual life.

Passions: Movements (neither good nor bad in themselves) of the sensitive appetite toward a real or apparent good, or away from a real or apparent evil.

Passive: When the soul or a faculty of man does not initiate some experience or action in the spiritual life, but is solely receptive to the action of God.

Purification: The counterpart to a growth in virtue, involving the rooting out of sin and all of its nuances, making greater room for the presence of God.

Additional Resources & Suggested Reading

For further reading about the life and spirituality of St. John of the Cross, we recommend:

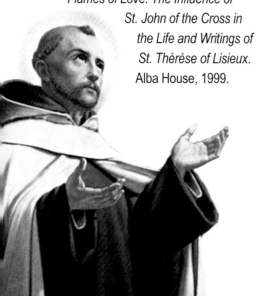

Dubay, Thomas. *Fire Within: St. Teresa of Avila, St. John of the Cross, and the Gospel On Prayer.* Ignatius Press, 1989.

Garrigou-Lagrange, Reginald. *Christian Perfection and Contemplation: According to St. Thomas Aquinas and St. John of the Cross.* TAN Books, 2003.

Gaucher, Guy. *John and Thérèse: Flames of Love: The Influence of St. John of the Cross in the Life and Writings of St. Thérèse of Lisieux.* Alba House, 1999.

St. John of the Cross, and Peers, E. Allison, tr. *Ascent of Mount Carmel.* Bottom of the Hill Publishing, 2010.

Bl. Pope John Paul II. *Master in the Faith: Apostolic Letter on the Fourth Centenary of the Death of St. John of the Cross, Doctor of the Church.* EWTN, http://www.ewtn.com/library/papaldoc/jpmaster.htm

St. Teresa of Avila. *The Autobiography of St. Teresa of Avila: The Life of St. Teresa of Jesus.* TAN Books, 1997.

St. Teresa of Avila. *The Interior Castle or the Mansions.* TAN Books, 2011.

St. Teresa of Avila. *The Way of Perfection.* TAN Books, 1997.